CHINESE MYTHOLOGY

Yudi
Jade Emperor

BY SAMANTHA S. BELL

CONTENT CONSULTANT
GANG LIU, PhD
ASSOCIATE TEACHING PROFESSOR
CARNEGIE MELLON UNIVERSITY

Kids Core
An Imprint of Abdo Publishing
abdobooks.com

Cover Photo: Pictures from History/Universal Images Group/Getty Images
Interior Photos: Pictures from History/Universal Images Group/Getty Images, 4–5; Shutterstock Images, 6, 9, 10, 11, 29 (top); CulturalEyes - AusGS2/Alamy, 12, 28 (top); Top Photo Corporation/Alamy, 14–15; Chintung Lee/Shutterstock Images, 16; MET/BOT/Alamy, 20–21; Rut Luecha/Shutterstock Images, 22; iStockphoto, 25; Jon Arnold Images Ltd/Alamy, 26, 29 (bottom); The History Collection/Alamy, 28 (bottom)

Editor: Ann Schwab
Series Designer: Ryan Gale

Library of Congress Control Number: 2022940685

Publisher's Cataloging-in-Publication Data

Names: Bell, Samantha S., author.
Title: Yudi: Jade Emperor / by Samantha S. Bell
Description: Minneapolis, Minnesota: Abdo Publishing, 2023 | Series: Chinese Mythology | Includes online resources and index.
Identifiers: ISBN 9781532199998 (lib. bdg.) | ISBN 9781098275198 (ebook)
Subjects: LCSH: Deities--Juvenile literature. | Gods, Chinese--Juvenile literature. | Mythology, Chinese--Juvenile literature.
Classification: DDC 299.51--dc23

CONTENTS

The Jade Emperor rules over the Heavenly Domain.

CHAPTER 1

The Great Race

Yudi, the Jade Emperor, is the supreme ruler of the heavens in Chinese mythology. He wanted to make a way to measure time for the people on Earth. He decided to separate time into years. That way, people could remember when they were born.

The zodiac animals are popular symbols in Chinese culture.

Yudi decided to name the years after different animals. To do this, he planned a great race between the animals. He would name a year after each of the first 12 animals that crossed the finish line. After 12 years, the cycle of names would start over again.

In one version of the story, the rat and the cat were friends. But when it was time for the race, the cat was taking a nap. The rat tried to wake up the cat, but the cat kept sleeping. So the rat chose the ox as its partner instead.

Chinese Zodiac

In the Chinese zodiac, each year is named after one of 12 animals. Some believe that people have the same traits as the animal of the year in which they were born. For example, someone born in the Year of the Tiger would be brave like a tiger.

During the race, the animals had to cross a river. The rat could not cross the river on its own, so the ox gave it a ride. Just before they reached the finish line, the rat jumped off and raced ahead. The rat came in first. So the Year of the Rat became the first of the 12 years in the Chinese zodiac.

Next came the ox, tiger, and rabbit. Then came the dragon, snake, horse, and goat. The last four to finish were the monkey, rooster, dog, and pig. The cat did not get included in the zodiac. It then became the enemy of the rat.

In China, 2022 was known as the Year of the Tiger.

The Chinese Zodiac

The Chinese zodiac assigns a specific animal to each year. The cycle is repeated every 12 years.

From across the Land

The story of the great race is a Chinese **myth**. Myths have been a part of Chinese culture for centuries. These types of stories have been told since at least 800 BCE. Some Chinese myths explain religious beliefs. Others describe places or historical figures. The myths come from all over China. They are shared as stories, poems, **chants**, and songs.

Yudi is often featured in the story of the great race. But in some versions of the story, he isn't included.

The myths include stories about animals, plants, dragons, and gods. There is often more than one version of a myth. There are different stories about the great race too. Sometimes the goat is replaced by a sheep or ram. Other times Yudi doesn't appear in the story. Other details might change as well. But each version tells the story about how measuring time began.

Explore Online

Visit the website below. Does it give you any new information about the great race that wasn't in Chapter One?

A Story in Mandarin: The Zodiac Animals

abdocorelibrary.com/yudi

13

Artwork featuring Yudi, *center*, can be found throughout China.

CHAPTER 2

From Prince to Emperor

Some myths about Yudi tell how he was born. There are many different stories. One legend tells the story of King Jingde and Queen Bao Yueguang. The king and queen did not have a son. They asked the priests to pray.

As the supreme ruler of the heavens, Yudi is sometimes called Heavenly Grandfather.

That night, the queen had a dream. She saw one of the highest-ranking gods riding on a dragon chariot. He had a boy in his arms. The queen begged the god for the child, and he gave her the boy. Then the dream ended. The next year, the queen had a baby boy, Yudi.

As he grew, the prince showed great kindness to the poor. When his father died, Yudi became king. But he gave up the throne and spent his life curing sickness and helping people. When his life ended, he became a god. His title is the Jade Emperor, and he rules over the Heavenly Domain.

A Heavenly Court

Yudi's powers in heaven are similar to those of emperors on Earth. Besides Yudi and his family, many other gods live in the Heavenly Domain. The important ones formed a court. Yudi rules over this court.

When the gods have disagreements, Yudi decides who is right. Like a human emperor, he commands armies, though his are made up of **spirits**. He can set his armies against anyone who offends him. Yudi is like the human rulers in another way. They sometimes can be tricked by others. Yudi can be outsmarted too.

In the 1500s CE, Wu Cheng'en wrote a novel featuring characters from Chinese myths, including the Jade Emperor:

> [Yudi was] surrounded by his immortal ministers on his throne in the Hall of Miraculous Mist in the Golden-gated Cloud Palace.

Source: Wu Cheng'en. *Journey to the West*. Translated by W. J. F. Jenner, Foreign Languages, 2003, p. 5.

Comparing Texts

Think about the quote. Does it support the information in this chapter? Or does it give a different perspective? Explain how in a few sentences.

The Kitchen God, *center*, watches over each family's activities.

CHAPTER 3

Celebrating with Yudi

Stories from China include gods on Earth too. Some of them protect villages, while others guard individual families. One is called the Kitchen God. Every family has their own Kitchen God guardian.

Yudi is honored beyond China. This temple to him is in Thailand.

They bring reports to Yudi about people's activities. Yudi considers each person's behavior. When people die, they then face a final judgment. Some who live perfect lives may become gods and goddesses.

Honoring the Emperor

Yudi is not always represented by a statue at his temples. Often there is only a tablet with his name on it. When there is an image of Yudi, he usually has a beard and is covered in gold. He sits on a throne, often holding a jade tablet. The image is placed on an altar as high as possible. Yudi may be alone or with statues of his children or other gods.

The Jade Emperor is still part of celebrations in China, including the Chinese New Year. In some homes, an image of the Kitchen God is placed in the kitchen. It watches all the activities in the home. On New Year's Day, the image is burned, and the god returns to heaven. He gives his report to Yudi. This report affects the family's good fortune for the year.

Not a Crown, but a *Mian*

When the Jade Emperor is depicted in art, he is usually wearing a special cap called a *mian*. It has a rectangular, flat top. Cords of beads hang from the front and back of the cap.

This statue of the Jade Emperor in Thailand shows him wearing a *mian*.

People light candles and burn incense to honor the
Jade Emperor on his birthday.

The Jade Emperor's birthday is the ninth day of the Chinese Lunar New Year. Festivals are held on the eighth and ninth days to celebrate. Feasts include meals with duck, chicken, and pork. Many people visit a temple of the Jade Emperor. They pray for health, safety, love, or money. Some people burn **incense**. They honor Yudi as the ruler of the heavens. They ask that he protect them and guide them through life.

LEGENDARY FACTS

Yudi, the Jade Emperor, is the supreme ruler of the Heavenly Domain.

He rules over a court of gods and makes decisions about disagreements.

Tiger
Rabbit
Ox
Dragon
Mouse
Snake
Pig
Horse
Dog
Goat
Rooster
Monkey
2022 2023
2033 2034 2035 2024
2045 2046 2047 2036
2032 2057 2048 2025
2044 2049 2037
2056 2050 2038 2026
2043 2051 2039
2035 2052 2027
2041 2040 2028
2031 2054 2053 2029
2042 2030

Yudi created the Chinese zodiac to help people measure years.

He is part of Chinese celebrations, including the New Year and his birthday.

Glossary

chants

songs that are sung repeating the same note throughout

incense

a substance that has a fragrant smell when burned

myth

a traditional story or legend that explains the history or cultural beliefs of a group of people

spirits

beings that are not of this world, such as ghosts or angels

virtues

right or good actions and thoughts

Online Resources

To learn more about Yudi and Chinese mythology, visit our free resource websites below.

Visit **abdocorelibrary.com** or scan this QR code for free Common Core resources for teachers and students, including vetted activities, multimedia, and booklinks, for deeper subject comprehension.

Visit **abdobooklinks.com** or scan this QR code for free additional online weblinks for further learning. These links are routinely monitored and updated to provide the most current information available.

Learn More

Chu, Eugenia. *Celebrating Chinese New Year*. Rockridge, 2021.

Wilhelm, Richard, and Frederick Martens. *Chinese Fairy Tales and Legends*. Bloomsbury China, 2019.

Index

About the Author

Samantha S. Bell lives in the foothills of the Blue Ridge Mountains with her family and lots of cats. She is the author of more than 130 nonfiction books for kids.